THE UNOFFICIAL

123

SESAME ST

LEGENDS
ALPHABET

Words by Robin Feiner

A is for **A**bby Cadabby. Abby the fairy-in-training arrived on Sesame Street with her wand, wings, pink fur, and pom-poms for ears. She speaks a language called "dragonfly," has her own fairy garden, and loves meeting new friends!

Bb

B is for Big Bird.
This eight-foot-tall yellow bird
has been on Sesame Street
since the first episode in 1969.
Curious and passionate about
knowledge, he helps us learn
too! According to the United
States Library of Congress,
Big Bird is a certified "Living
Legend!"

C is for Cookie Monster. The world-famous wild blue monster with googly eyes and a growly voice! You know him as Cookie Monster, and he's got a sweet tooth for cookies. He's learned valuable lessons about sharing them with friends, and that they are a "sometimes food."

D is for **D**on Music.
Don Music is Sesame Street's resident piano player and composer. He often suffers from writer's block — but he finds encouragement and inspiration with help from friends like Kermit!

TICKLE

TICKLE

Ee

E is for **El**mo.
Elmo is the famous fluffy red monster and beloved face of Sesame Street! He has his own talk show — The Not-Too-Late Show with Elmo. As an embodiment of love, Elmo enjoys kisses, cuddles, and tickles!
"La la la la, Elmo's World!"

Ff

F is for Friends: Bert and Ernie. Sesame Street is all about friends, and there's no better companionship than Bert and Ernie's. Easy-going Ernie and uptight Bert are the classic odd couple, but their differences always help solve their problems.

G is for Grover.
This furry blue fella is
always eager to help ...
but he's comically bad at it!
He has a wild imagination,
and his alter-ego, Super
Grover, is Sesame Street's
local legendary superhero.

H is for The Honkers.
With squeezable noses and
horns for ears, The Honkers
are a fuzzy family who talk
by — you guessed it —
honking! They regularly
feature in songs and even
have one named after their
unique talent: "Honk
Around the Clock."

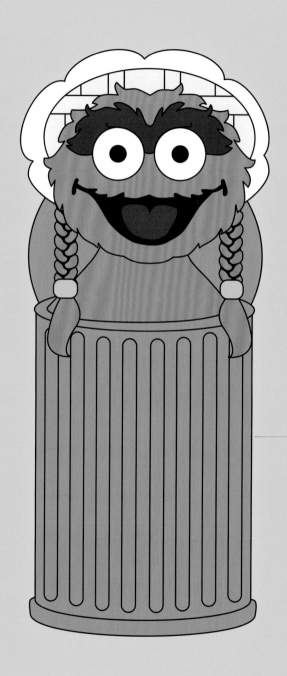

Ii

I is for Irvine.
Oscar the Grouch's little
niece, Irvine, is the screaming
green grouch in a bonnet.
Her wild tantrums teach poor
old Oscar to be patient as he
tries to soothe her and meet
her demands.

Jj

J is for Julia.

When this four-year-old Muppet with Autism came to Sesame Street, she quickly became friends with Elmo, Zoe, and Abby. Julia helps us understand that people with autism aren't so different from the rest of us. What a legend!

**K is for Kermit.
It's not easy being green,
but Kermit the Frog has made
it work. His illustrious careers
as a TV show host, crooning
singer, and hard-hitting
reporter might explain why
Kermit has a star on the
Hollywood Walk of Fame!**

Fix-It Shop

L is for Luis.
As two of the show's longest-running stars, Luis and his wife, Maria, lived on Sesame Street for forty-four years. They ran the Fix-It Shop, where they mended toasters and a lot of problems the local monsters had!

Mm

M is for Mama Bear.
Based on Goldilocks and
the Three Bears, Mama
Bear and her family began
appearing on Sesame Street
in the early 90s. Nowadays,
she's the drummer and
bandleader of "Mama Bear
and the Monsters" on The
Not-Too-Late Show with Elmo!

N is for Mr. **N**oodle. Appearing in Elmo's World, Mr. Noodle is regularly called on by Elmo to solve problems. He's a funny mime with a bushy mustache, gigantic bowtie, and baggy trousers. His trial and error approach helps him find the answers!

O is for **O**scar the Grouch. We all know the fuzzy green grump living in a trash can with his pal Slimey the Worm! As a Sesame Street staple, his grouchy attitude has highlighted important traits like understanding and tolerance for over fifty years.

P is for Prairie Dawn. Prairie Dawn — a six-year-old Muppet and born entertainer — loves singing, playing piano, and organizing pageants for her friends. She regularly serves as Sesame Street's correspondent in various news slots on the show!

Q is for The **Q**ueens. Many Queens have graced Sesame Street with their honor over the years. From the caring Queen Quinella to the Queen of Nacho Picchu to the Queen who built a recycled castle for her daughter, the Princess — they're all royal legends!

Rr

R is for **Rosita.**
Sweet Rosita is the winged turquoise monster hailing from a Mexican cave! The brilliant bilingual guitar player adds Latin flavor to Sesame Street and regularly presents the Spanish Word of the Day.

S is for **S**nuffy.
Snuffy — aka Mr. Aloysius Snuffleupagas — is a shaggy mammoth-type monster and Big Bird's best friend. For a long-time, residents thought he was imaginary ... until they finally met him. After that, he quickly became part of the Sesame Street family!

T is for **Telly.**
This adorable pink monster with an orange nose is a worrywart who needs constant reassurance to be confident! As his name suggests, Telly is obsessed with television. He also loves triangles!

U is for **U**ncle Wally.
Uncle Wally is the bowtie-wearing uncle of Bob, Sesame Street's music teacher. As a traveling salesman, he visited Bob and Sesame Street regularly. Wally was always ready to share a goofy gag or a tall tale from his travels!

V is for Count von Count. Count von Count is obsessed with counting and loves numbers! A parody of another famous vampire legend, Count Dracula, this iconic purple Muppet has the same fanged smile, pointy ears, thick Transylvanian accent, and villainous laugh — "Mwahaha!"

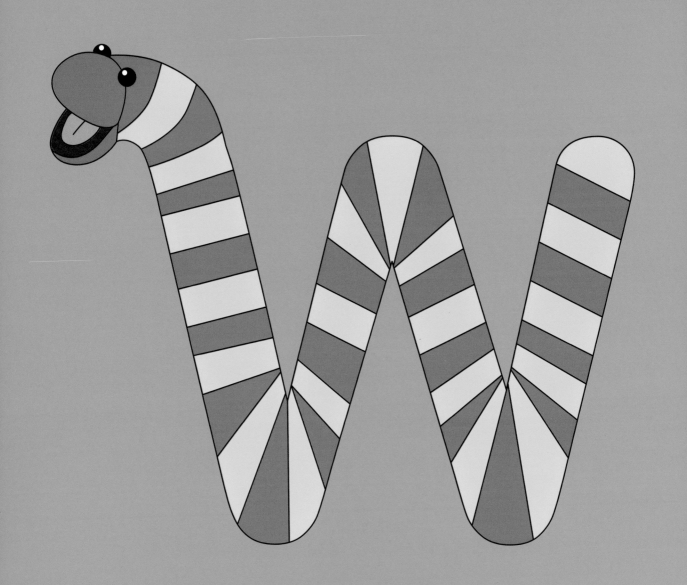

Ww

W is for Slimey the Worm
As adorable as he is slimy,
this tiny orange and yellow
worm is Oscar's pet. He lives
in Oscar's trash can, plays the
tuba and clarinet, and legend
has it he was the first worm
on the moon!

X is for Ro**X**ie Marie
A smart young Muppet originally from Brooklyn, Roxie Marie acts like a big sister to Elmo. But like any little brother, Elmo often gets in her way of pursuing creepy-crawly friends: bugs and butterflies!

Y is for **Y**ip Yips.
With their googly eyes, antennas, and big mouths, these Martians are named after the noise they make: "Yip-Yip-Yip!" Since floating down from outer space, they've been curious and easily scared by devices like toasters, clocks, and ringing telephones!

Zz

Z is for Zoe.
This delightful three-year-old yellow monster is friends with fellow legend Elmo. She's often dressed in a tutu because she loves to sing and perform ballet. It should come as no surprise that her favorite letter is Z!

The ever-expanding legendary library

EXPLORE THESE LEGENDARY ALPHABETS & MORE AT WWW.ALPHABETLEGENDS.COM

SESAME ST LEGENDS ALPHABET
www.alphabetlegends.com

Published by Alphabet Legends Pty Ltd in 2021
Created by Beck Feiner
Copyright © Alphabet Legends Pty Ltd 2021

9780645200157

Printed and bound in China.